Cats Are Good Company

Cats Are Good Company

by Ursula Landshoff

Harper & Row, Publishers

An I CAN READ Book
about owning a cat

Library of Congress Cataloging in Publication Data
Landshoff, Ursula.
  Cats are good company.

  (An I can read book)
  Summary: Discusses where to find and how to
choose a cat, and how to care for it when you
take it home.
  1. Cats—Juvenile literature.   [1. Cats]
I. Title. II. Series.
SF445.7.L36 1983   636.8   82-48844
ISBN 0-06-023676-0
ISBN 0-06-023677-9 (lib. bdg.)

CONTENTS

Cats are good company.

You can talk to them.

They will listen to you

and keep your secrets.

Take good care of your cat.

She will love you

if you treat her right.

A cat does not like

to walk on a leash like a dog.

A cat has a mind of her own.

She likes to go out to explore.

She will come back to you by herself.

House cats keep your house cozy.

On a cold night

your cat may jump into your bed.

She will purr loudly

and snuggle up to you.

In a minute

you will both feel warm.

She may share

your bed for a while.

Ask your family

if you can have a cat

before you try to find one.

13

Would you like one with a black face?

Or a white face?

A striped cat

or an orange cat?

A cat with long hair or short hair?

You must brush a cat

with long hair every day.

This will keep her tidy and healthy.

A soft brush and a metal comb

are good for this.

You should not

give a cat a bath

except in special cases.

A cat needs the oil

in her coat.

Do you want a kitten

or a grown-up cat?

A kitten is more fun.

But a kitten needs more care.

In a few months

the kitten will be grown up, too.

girl cat   tomcat

Do you want a tomcat or a girl cat?

If you look under its tail,

you can tell if a kitten is

a girl cat

or a tomcat.

19

You can get cats in many places.

Some people get them in stores.

Others get them from friends

or from animal shelters.

20

One boy got his cat for a quarter

at a fair in the country.

Sometimes a cat finds you.

Before you take your cat home,

bring her to an animal doctor.

She will need shots.

23

Ask the doctor to tell you

what to feed your cat

and how much to feed her.

Cats love fish and meat.

But chicken bones and fish bones

can make them very sick.

Make sure that they do not get any.

A cat needs water.

Make sure there is always some

in her bowl.

Sometimes you can give her milk

for a treat.

Give your cat three different dishes:

one for water,

one for solid food,

one for milk.

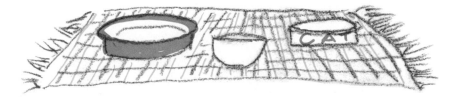

Always put her dishes

in the same spot.

Don't carry your cat in your arms
when you are bringing her home.
A cat is curious.
She might try to wiggle away from you.
Get a cardboard box to carry her in.
Punch air holes in the box
so the cat can breathe.

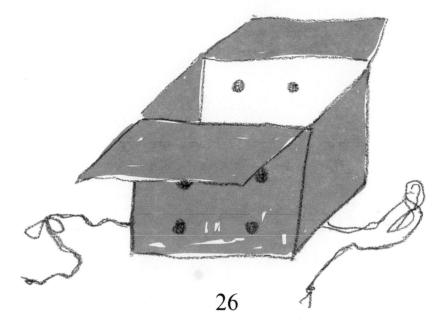

You can also go to a pet store

and buy a case with a view.

27

When you put the cat into the box,
pick her up gently.
Put both hands
around her chest.

When you carry her,
put one hand under
her back legs.

Don't ever grab a cat suddenly.

She may be shy in the beginning.

She might get frightened
and try to get away.
She may scratch you.

Let her go if she gets nervous.

Leave her alone for a moment

until she quiets down.

When you get your cat home,

let her jump out of the box

by herself.

Introduce her to your family

and friends quietly.

No pushing or shoving!

Make a bed for your kitten
in a warm corner.

Remember, she used to sleep

curled up with

all her brothers and sisters.

A basket filled with shredded paper

is a cozy bed for a kitten.

33

When she feels at home,

she will sleep in a spot

she likes best.

Cats are clean animals.

They like to get

into the habit of things.

Put a box with cat litter

in a corner

of the bathroom.

Put the cat into the box

the same day

you bring her home.

Hold one of her front legs

and scratch the litter with it.

She will soon understand

what you want her to do.

After a few times

she will go to the box by herself.

Clean the box every day.

Put in new litter twice a week.

Cats love to scratch.

Your cat needs a scratching post.

Put her in front of the post.

Take one of her front paws

and help her scratch.

She will get the feeling of it.

She will learn quickly

what the post is for.

Say "NO" in a loud voice

if she scratches the furniture.

Pick her up and put her

in front of the post.

She will get the idea.

Make sure the cat doesn't scratch

your baby brother or sister.

Don't let the cat play

in the baby's room.

Your mother or father can

put up a screen door

to keep the cat out.

If you live in an apartment,

close the windows and doors

when you go out.

A cat is nosy.

She might go out

and get herself into trouble.

She can hurt herself badly

if she jumps out a window.

Cats sleep a lot while you are out.

But they have built-in clocks.

If you come home

at the same time every day,

your cat will be waiting for you.

She may be hiding when you come in.

She may jump out and surprise you.

She will try to help you

do your homework.

Cats love to play

with anything that moves.

They will chase flies, or bees,

or butterflies.

A young kitten

does not know

that she is chasing

a tasty meal.

She may have fun with goldfish, too,

even if she cannot catch them.

She dips her paw in the water.

She cools off and cleans herself.

It is best to keep your plants

away from your cat.

A cat will nibble on house plants.

Some plants can make cats very sick.

46

A cat likes to be spoiled.

Or to spoil you.

Cats love to climb trees.

A tree makes a good lookout.

A cat can watch other furry animals,

and ones with feathers, too.

Don't climb after your cat.

She will come down

when she gets hungry.

She will be happy

if you have water ready for her.

She may even be happy enough

to let you scratch her

behind the ears.

Once in a while

a cat may not have fun outside.

She may come home

with red, swollen eyes.

She may be the smelliest cat

in the neighborhood.

She chased a skunk

and the skunk won.

She will ask you for help.

She will try to tell you

she will never chase a skunk again.

Fill a large plastic tub
with tomato juice.
Soak the cat in the tub.

Rinse her off quickly.

Dry the cat well with a big towel.

Keep her warm.

She may be a little pink

under the chin.

But she will still be the same cat.

Don't give your cat

toys with loose parts

or sharp edges

that can hurt her.

A soft rubber toy

is not a good toy.

Your cat can bite off

a piece of rubber.

If she swallows it,

she can get very sick.

A tennis ball is better.

You can also make your own toy.

Tie a piece of paper on a string.

Your cat will chase this paper mouse.

A cat in the house

will keep the mice away.

A mouse inside the house will hide

when it smells a cat around.

But once in her lifetime

your cat may surprise you.

She will catch a mouse or a bird

and proudly bring it to you.

Don't scold her.

She wants to make you happy.

If you don't like her gift,

just turn away.

CAN YOU HAVE A CAT
AND A DOG?

A cat and a dog

can become good friends.

It is best

to get them used to each other

when the cat is young.

A kitten cannot hurt the dog.

Her claws are still too short

to scratch badly.

The dog has a chance to learn

to protect himself.

Feed the cat and the dog

in different rooms.

Or put the cat's food up

in a high place.

A cat will never share her food

with a dog.

Do you want more cats?

If you do not "fix" your girl cat,
one day you may find her
with a new family of kittens
in your closet.

Now it is time

to look for people

who need cats.

If you don't want more cats,

take your cat to an animal doctor.

He will do a simple operation

so your cat cannot have kittens.